NEW HORIZONS

EXPLORING JUPITER, PLUTO, AND BEYOND

By John Hamilton

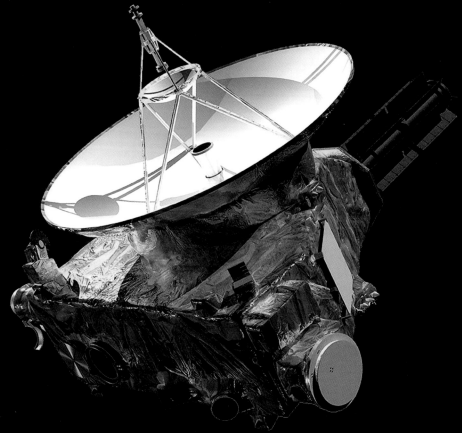

D1606739

XTREME SPACECRAFT

A&D Xtreme
An imprint of Abdo Publishing | abdopublishing.com

abdopublishing.com

Published by Abdo Publishing, a division of ABDO, PO Box 398166, Minneapolis, Minnesota 55439. Copyright ©2018 by Abdo Consulting Group, Inc. International copyrights reserved in all countries. No part of this book may be reproduced in any form without written permission from the publisher. A&D Xtreme™ is a trademark and logo of Abdo Publishing.

Printed in the United States of America, North Mankato, MN.
042017
052017

Editor: Sue Hamilton
Graphic Design: Sue Hamilton
Cover Design: Candice Keimig
Cover Photo: iStock
Interior Images: All photos and illustrations NASA, except page 14 photo by Vince Bly.

Websites
To learn more about Xtreme Spacecraft, visit abdobooklinks.com.
These links are routinely monitored and updated to provide the most current information available.

Publisher's Cataloging-in-Publication Data

Names: Hamilton, John, author.
Title: New horizons: exploring Jupiter, Pluto, and beyond / by John Hamilton.
Other titles: Exploring Jupiter, Pluto, and beyond
Description: Minneapolis, MN : Abdo Publishing, 2018. | Series: Xtreme spacecraft | Includes index.
Identifiers: LCCN 2016962227 | ISBN 9781532110108 (lib. bdg.) | ISBN 9781680787955 (ebook)
Subjects: LCSH: Jupiter (Planet)--Exploration--Juvenile literature. | Pluto (Planet)--Exploration--Juvenile literature. | Outer space--Exploration--Juvenile literature.
Classification: DDC 523--dc23
LC record available at http://lccn.loc.gov/2016962227

CONTENTS

EXPLORING JUPITER, PLUTO, AND BEYOND

NASA's New Horizons spacecraft flew past Pluto on July 14, 2015. It traveled through space for almost 3 billion miles (4.8 billion km) to reach the icy dwarf planet.

New Horizons
Spacecraft

It took stunning photos and collected priceless scientific data. Thanks to New Horizons, scientists are now beginning to unlock the secrets of faraway Pluto and the history of the solar system.

Charon,
Pluto's Largest Moon

Pluto

MYSTERIOUS PLUTO

Scientists call Pluto a dwarf planet. Like the eight major planets of the solar system, it is round and orbits the Sun. However, it is very small. It is made of ice and rock. It is just one-sixth the mass of Earth's Moon. Pluto was discovered in 1930. It is named after the Roman god of the dead.

Pluto

XTREME FACT – *An aluminum canister attached to New Horizons contains a portion of the ashes of Clyde Tombaugh, the American astronomer who discovered Pluto in 1930. Tombaugh died in 1997 at the age of 90.*

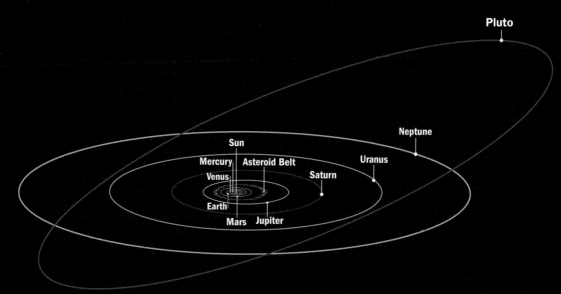

Pluto has a tilted, elliptical orbit. It takes 248 Earth years for it to circle the Sun. Pluto is only 1,473 miles (2,371 km) in diameter. There is only about one-fifteenth the gravity on Pluto as there is on Earth.

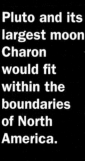

Pluto and its largest moon Charon would fit within the boundaries of North America.

Pluto is extremely cold. Far from the warming rays of the Sun, its average temperature is about minus 382 degrees Fahrenheit (-230°C).

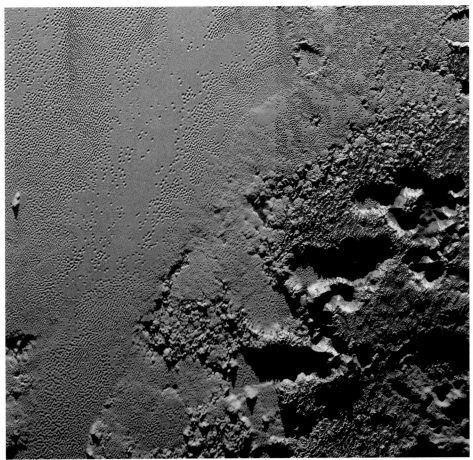

A photo from the New Horizons spacecraft shows a portion of the frozen plains and rugged highlands of Pluto's icy southeastern area.

PLANNING AND BUILDING

NASA began planning New Horizons in the early 2000s. Astronomers wanted to study Pluto. It was the last unexplored planet of the solar system. (After New Horizons was launched, scientists in 2006 downgraded Pluto's status to "dwarf planet.")

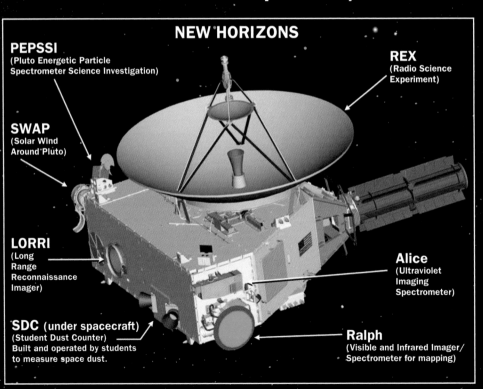

NEW HORIZONS

PEPSSI
(Pluto Energetic Particle Spectrometer Science Investigation)

REX
(Radio Science Experiment)

SWAP
(Solar Wind Around Pluto)

LORRI
(Long Range Reconnaissance Imager)

Alice
(Ultraviolet Imaging Spectrometer)

SDC (under spacecraft)
(Student Dust Counter)
Built and operated by students to measure space dust.

Ralph
(Visible and Infrared Imager/ Spectrometer for mapping)

New Horizons planning included cameras, mapping instruments, and many scientific pieces of equipment that would provide information about Pluto.

PLUTO AND ITS FIVE MOONS

Pluto

Styx

Hydra

Nix

Charon

Kerberos

During its flyby, New Horizons would also investigate Pluto's five moons. From there, the spacecraft would travel farther into the mysterious Kuiper belt.

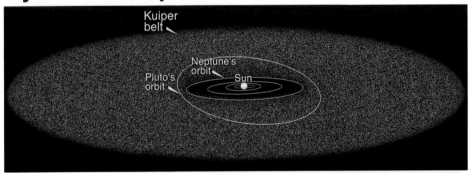

Kuiper belt

Neptune's orbit

Pluto's orbit

Sun

XTREME FACT – The Kuiper belt is a part of the solar system that starts just beyond the orbit of the planet Neptune and extends billions of miles outward. It looks like a large, donut-shaped disk, with the sun in the center. It is filled with objects such as asteroids and dwarf planets, including Pluto.

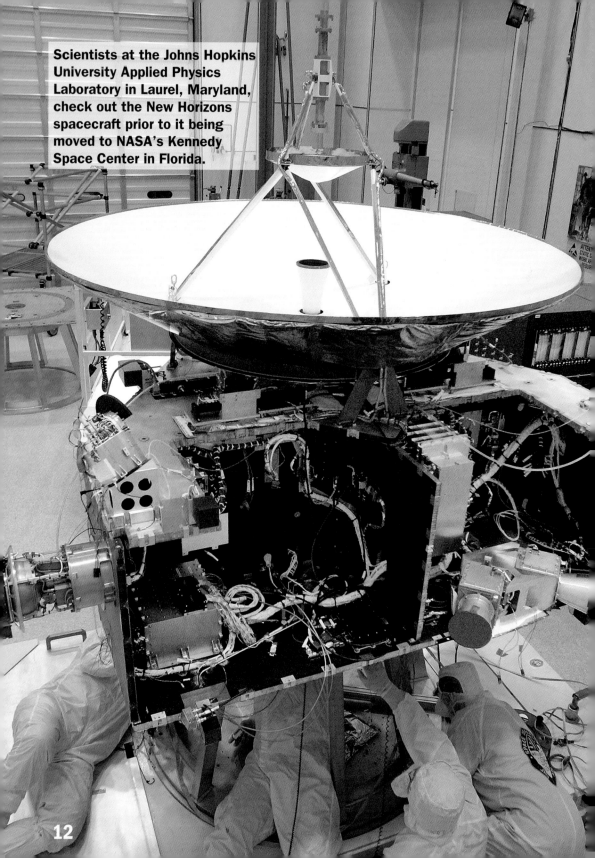

Scientists at the Johns Hopkins University Applied Physics Laboratory in Laurel, Maryland, check out the New Horizons spacecraft prior to it being moved to NASA's Kennedy Space Center in Florida.

In 2005, the piano-sized New Horizons spacecraft arrived for testing at NASA's Kennedy Space Center in Florida. It carries seven science instruments. They include sensitive cameras, plus devices to measure the atmosphere of Pluto and its moons. Also on board are devices that measure the solar wind around Pluto and dust particles in space. In December 2005, the spacecraft passed its final tests. It was ready to launch.

New Horizons is prepared for launch at NASA's Kennedy Space Center.

XTREME FACT – New Horizons is powered by nuclear fuel. Its radioisotope thermoelectric generator uses plutonium-238. It generates slightly less than 250 watts of electricity. That is barely enough to light two bright light bulbs, but it is enough to power all of the spacecraft's electronic systems.

LAUNCH

New Horizons was launched on January 19, 2006, at Cape Canaveral Air Force Station in Florida. It was carried into space aboard a powerful Atlas V rocket.

It was the fastest spacecraft to ever leave the Earth. It entered space at more than 36,000 miles per hour (57,936 kph). After a perfect launch, New Horizons began its nine-year journey to the edge of the solar system.

XTREME FACT – The Atlas V rocket used for the New Horizons spacecraft was a three-stage launch vehicle. With New Horizons aboard, the Atlas V at launch weighed about 1.26 million pounds (571,526 kg).

JUPITER ENCOUNTER

In February 2007, New Horizons passed within 1.4 million miles (2.3 million km) of the planet Jupiter. That was close enough to the gas giant to receive a gravity boost. The spacecraft's speed increased to 51,000 miles per hour (82,077 kph).

An illustration shows New Horizons during its flyby past Jupiter and the planet's moon, Io, in 2007.

 XTREME FACT – Without Jupiter's gravity boost, New Horizons would have needed an extra three years to reach Pluto.

During the flyby, New Horizons took images and scientific readings. It also studied several of Jupiter's 67 moons. On the moon Io, scientists were startled to see the plume of an active volcano. It spewed material 205 miles (330 km) above the moon's surface.

New Horizons captured a volcanic explosion on Io, Jupiter's third-largest moon.

PLUTO FLYBY

New Horizons arrived near Pluto after a nine-year, 3-billion-mile (4.8-billion-km) journey. It came closest to the dwarf planet on July 14, 2015. When it sped by, it was just 7,750 miles (12,472 km) from Pluto.

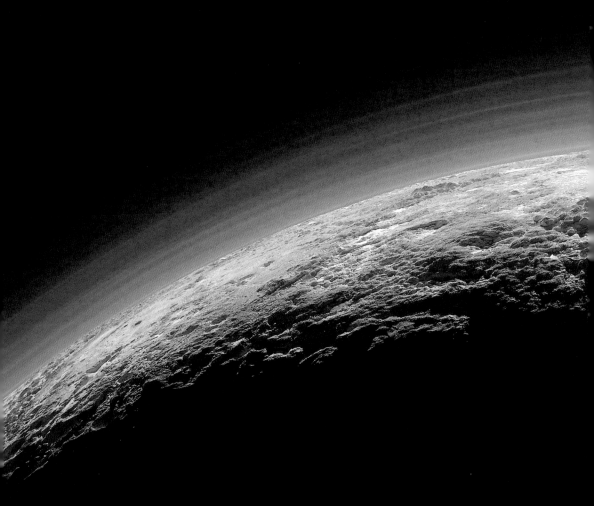

For several months before and after the flyby, the spacecraft's cameras and other science instruments recorded many gigabytes of data.

XTREME FACT – *About a week before the Pluto flyby, the computer aboard New Horizons experienced a software failure. The spacecraft automatically switched to its backup computer and awaited instructions from NASA. Much to their relief, scientists were soon able to fix the problem.*

XTREME FACT – *New Horizons uses a main computer that is protected against the harmful radiation in space. The spacecraft uses a version of the MIPS R3000 central processing unit (CPU) used in the original PlayStation game console. Although not very speedy, it is a very stable and hardy CPU.*

The cameras on New Horizons captured detailed images of Pluto. The spacecraft was so far from Earth that it took 4.5 hours for radio messages—traveling at the speed of light—to reach home. When data and photos were finally received, scientists were amazed at the new surface details they saw. They also learned about Pluto's thin, layered atmosphere, which includes a haze of nitrogen, methane, and carbon monoxide gasses.

New Horizons photographed a snakeskin-looking Pluto landscape on July 14, 2015. The vast rippling ridges, called Tartarus Dorsa, stretched for hundreds of miles.

Thanks to New Horizons, we know that Pluto has a young surface that is geologically active. There are steep mountains made of ice. One heart-shaped region is nearly 1,000 miles (1,609 km) across. It is named Tombaugh Regio, in honor of Pluto's discoverer. It is mostly smooth and made of frozen nitrogen, carbon dioxide, and methane ice.

Pluto

Tombaugh Regio

The Tombaugh Regio is known as the "heart" of Pluto.

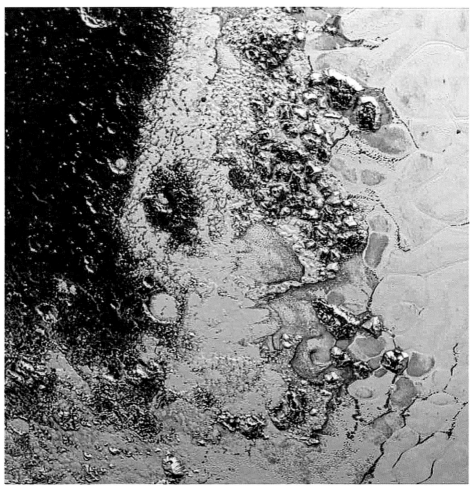

NASA scientists discovered a mountain range on the southwest border of Pluto's heart-shaped Tombaugh Regio on July 14, 2015. Photographed by New Horizons' Long Range Reconnaissance Imager (LORRI), the mountains lie between bright, icy plains and a dark, heavily cratered area.

XTREME FACT – Only four other spacecraft—all from the United States—flew farther than New Horizons. They include Pioneer 10, Pioneer 11, Voyager 1, and Voyager 2. Voyager 1, which launched in 1977, has left the solar system, venturing into interstellar space between the stars.

Pluto is about two-thirds rock and one-third ice. It may have ice volcanoes. Instead of spewing hot lava, they release a slush of frozen water, nitrogen, and methane.

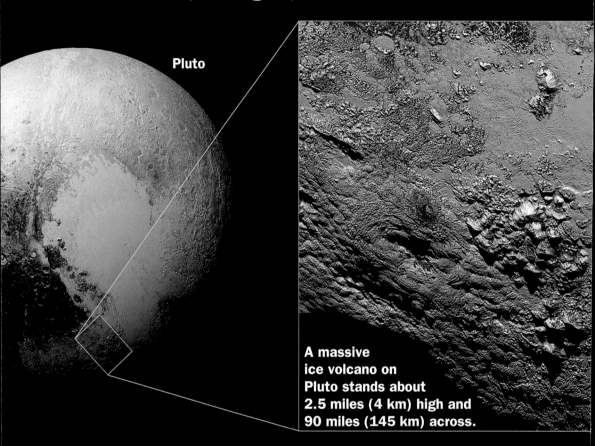

Pluto

A massive
ice volcano on
Pluto stands about
2.5 miles (4 km) high and
90 miles (145 km) across.

XTREME FACT – New Horizons has a large radio dish antenna, but the spacecraft can only transmit less than two kilobytes of data per second. A single high-resolution image can take longer than 30 minutes to send. It wasn't until October 2016 that New Horizons sent all its information from the Pluto flyby.

Near Pluto's equator is a mountain range. It is made of huge blocks of water ice. The mountains rise nearly 11,000 feet (3,353 m). They probably formed less than 100,000 years ago. That is young for a mountain range. Pluto is probably still building its surface.

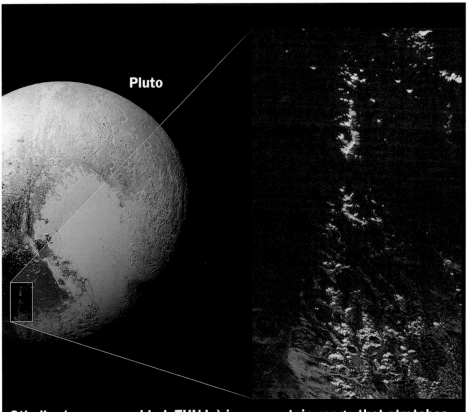

Pluto

Cthulhu (pronounced kuh-THU-lu) is a mountain range that stretches nearly halfway around Pluto's equator. Measuring about 1,850 miles (2,977 km) long and 450 miles (724 km) wide, Cthulhu is slightly larger than the state of Alaska.

PLUTO'S MOONS

During its flyby, New Horizons examined Pluto's five moons. The largest moon is called Charon. The others include Nix, Hydra, Kerberos, and Styx.

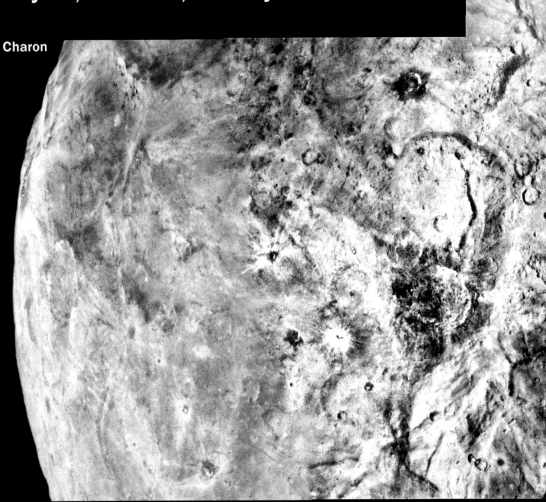

Charon

Pluto's moons were probably formed billions of years ago. A large object, perhaps another dwarf planet, collided with Pluto. The collision resulted in debris that eventually combined and formed Pluto's moons.

XTREME FACT – *Charon has steep cliffs and deep canyons. One canyon is more than 600 miles (966 km) long. Another is between 4 and 6 miles (6.4 to 9.7 km) deep. There are very few ancient meteor impact craters. These clues tell astronomers that Charon's fractured crust is relatively young, and is still actively forming.*

THE MISSION CONTINUES

After the Pluto flyby, New Horizons flew deeper into the Kuiper belt. It used much of its remaining hydrazine fuel to change course. Its destination is a large, rocky object named 2014 MU_{69}. It is about four billion miles (6.4 billion km) from Earth.

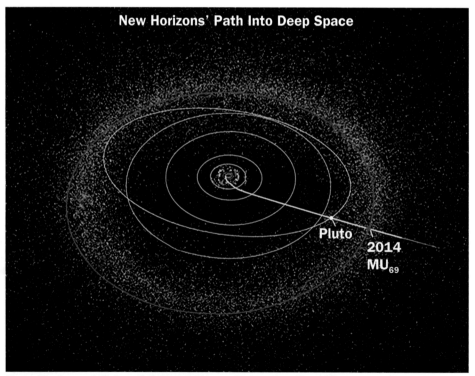

New Horizons' flyby of 2014 MU_{69} will be the first time a spacecraft explores an object discovered *after* the craft left Earth.

The New Horizons spacecraft should start studying 2014 MU$_{69}$ in late 2018. If successful, the extended mission will help astronomers understand the mysteries of the Kuiper belt, and how our solar system was first formed.

A NASA illustration shows a New Horizons flyby of a Kuiper belt object (KBO).

XTREME FACT – After its extended mission studying Kuiper belt objects, New Horizons will eventually run out of power and lose contact with Earth. The intrepid little probe will then drift into interstellar space, far beyond our solar system.

GLOSSARY

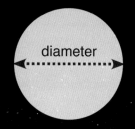

DIAMETER
The distance through the center of
an object, from one side to the other.

ELLIPTICAL ORBIT
An orbit that is oval shaped. Pluto has an elliptical
orbit. The eight major planets in our solar system
have mostly round orbits, all on the same plane.
In addition to being elliptical, Pluto's orbit is also
tilted, on a different plane. Pluto's elliptical orbit
means it is not always the same distance from the
sun. Sometimes in its orbit, it is actually slightly
closer to the sun than the planet Neptune. At other
points, it is much, much farther away.

FLYBY
When a spacecraft travels close to a planet or other
object but does not enter into an orbit around it.
During a flyby, a spacecraft has one chance to take
as many photos and gather as much scientific data
as possible before it sails on to its next destination.

GIGABYTE
A unit of digital information equal to one billion
bytes. It is often used to measure the amount
of information held by computer hard drives
or solid state drives (SSDs).

HYDRAZINE
A toxic, flammable liquid sometimes used in rocket fuel, or as a propellant for spacecraft thrusters.

MASS
The amount of matter that an object contains. Many people confuse mass and weight. Weight is the amount of force exerted by gravity on an object. The more massive an object is, the more it is affected by gravity, and the heavier it is. For example, a lead cannonball has more mass than a baseball. On Earth, the cannonball weighs more than the baseball because it is more affected by Earth's gravity. However, in space, away from Earth's gravity, both objects have virtually no weight. But the cannonball always has more mass than the baseball.

PLUTONIUM-238
A highly radioactive element that produces heat. The heat is converted to electricity in a radioisotope power system, such as the one used on the New Horizons spacecraft. This system is more reliable than solar panels. Radioisotope power systems produce steady, uninterrupted amounts of electricity, often for decades.

SOLAR WIND
Streams of charged particles that are given off by stars. Solar wind is a plasma of electrons, protons, and other particles. They are so energetic they can escape the Sun's gravity.

INDEX

New Horizons'
final view of
Pluto.